Searching For GOD After DRIFTING AWAY

Odella Glenn

Copyright © 2017 by Odella Glenn

Searching For GOD
After Drifting Away
by Odella Glenn

Printed in the United States of America.

ISBN 9781545600122

All rights reserved solely by the author. The author guarantees all contents are original and do not infringe upon the legal rights of any other person or work. No part of this book may be reproduced in any form without the permission of the author. The views expressed in this book are not necessarily those of the publisher.

Scripture quotations taken from the New King James Version (NKJV). Copyright © 1979, 1980, 1982 by Thomas Nelson, Inc. Used by permission. All rights reserved.

Scripture quotations taken from the Holy Bible, New Living Translation (NLT). Copyright © 1996 by Tyndale House Foundation. Used by permission of Tyndale House Publishers, Inc.

Scripture quotations taken from The Message (MSG). Copyright © 2002. Used by permission of NavPress Publishing Group. Used by permission. All rights reserved.

Scripture quotations taken from the Holy Bible, New International Version (NIV). Copyright © 1973, 1978, 1984 by International Bible Society. Used by permission. All rights reserved.

Edited by Xulon Press.

www.xulonpress.com

TABLE OF CONTENTS

Dedication vii
Acknowledgments ix
Foreword xi
Endorsement xiii
Introduction xv

1. Searching for God 21
2. Hearing God's Voice 30
3. Halloween Tricks and the Divine Treat 37
4. The Lost Keys 41
5. Droopy, Withered Plants on Assignment 46
6. Parable of the Lost Gloves 50
7. The Bird Connections 55
8. Led by the Holy Spirit 60
9. God Communicates through Dreams 68
10. Falls —after Age Fifty 77
Sinner's Prayer 83
About the Author 85

DEDICATION

To the memory of my parents and ancestors who laid a solid Christian foundation to follow.

To the memory of my deceased family members with whom I had a remarkable relationship: father, George Dove; husband, Carl Glenn; son, Emery Glenn.

To Crystal Glenn, my daughter/"Mama" and best friend; Maria Glenn, my daughter-in-law; my grandchildren, Idris, Emery, Jamila, Crystal and Jasmin; my great-grandchildren, Mia and Ethan.

ACKNOWLEDGMENTS

I am grateful for cherished family and friends who encourage me to keep my writing dream alive.

Expressing appreciation for prophetess Lois Tyler, for it is under her tutelage I am born again and again.

Thanks to Daughters of Zion Ministries and Bible study class, through which spiritual relationships have evolved and prayers, support and encouragement abound.

FOREWORD

Searching for God after Drifting Away is a wonderful book of short testimonies of the writer's personal experiences that are all biblically based. These stories are exciting, encouraging and informative and will leave a lasting impression on your heart.

In this church age and time in our country, it is refreshing to hear an open, transparent message that causes you to do an inner search about your relationship with our Savior Jesus. It will bring conviction to unbelievers to call on Jesus as Lord and Savior.

Time is too short to play-act as a Christian. It is time to become a right-now Christian who faces truth and doesn't trade it off for comfort. This book demonstrates Odella Glenn's candid ability to express biblical truths that will liberate all.

If you need an uplift in your faith, I suggest reading this book, *Searching for God after Drifting Away,* to close the gap of wandering.

Mrs. Glenn, thank you for your love for God and His people enough to be so transparent. The Lord's continued blessing in your intimate relationship with Him.

Prophetess Lois Tyler

Pastor, The Reconciled Church

Southfield, Michigan

ENDORSEMENT

When I was asked to edit this marvelous book by author Odella Glenn, the thought never occurred to me that I would find myself traveling down memory lane. But that's what happened....

It was 1976, and I was a faithful little "churchgoer" busy making pies and telling lies. I was even the church's announcement clerk and, believe it or not, a Sunday school teacher! I think I got the job because I could read—not because I was saved. In fact, I got saved while leading a lost soul to Christ. To tell the truth, I was an unsaved evangelist. Fast forward forty years....

It is now 2016, and, as I look back over my life, I can see how I wasn't much different from many of my family, friends and associates. Church was something we did on Sunday for various reasons, none of them righteous.

Maybe you can relate to what I am saying. Did you go because your parents told you to? Did you go to impress the neighbors? Did you go to meet that boyfriend, girlfriend, wife or husband? Business connection? Whatever your reason might have been, the plain and simple question Odella Glenn is asking is this: Are you a Christian? Do you have a personal relationship with Jesus Christ? Or do you have a second-hand relationship based on what you heard and not what you experienced?

Friends, when you come before the Lord Jesus Christ on judgment day, will you hear Him say, "Well done, my good and faithful servant," or will you hear Him say, "Depart from Me. I know you not"?

Did you ever have a personal relationship with Jesus Christ? Perhaps you once did but have drifted away. Now is the time for you to get so close to Him that you can hear His heartbeat. That's what Mrs. Glenn in *Searching for God after Drifting Away* is encouraging you to do. She found her way, and so can you.

"I have heard of thee by the hearing of the ear: but now mine eye seeth thee" (Job 42:5).

Dr. Mary D. Edwards, Leaves of Gold Consulting, www.leavesofgoldconsulting.com

Introduction

Research indicates that "The United States remains home to more Christians than any other country in the world, and a large majority of Americans—roughly seven in ten—continue to identify with some branch of the Christian faith." (*"America's Changing Religious Landscape"* Pew Research Center, Washington, D.C. (May 12, 2015). www.Pewforum.org). Are you a Christian?

Merriam-Webster's dictionary defines Christian as "a person who believes in the teachings of Jesus Christ." The word "Christian" can be summed up biblically as someone who is a follower of Jesus Christ. As a Christian, you expect to go to heaven when your earthly journey ends and spend eternity there with God, right? Not so fast! Did you know that all those who profess Christianity are *not* going to heaven? Jesus said so. "Not everyone who says to me, "Lord, Lord," will enter the kingdom of heaven, but only he who does the will of my Father" (Matthew 7:21). In other words, a person can "believe" in the teachings of Jesus Christ but not "do" the teachings of Jesus Christ, even though he may call Jesus "Lord." James 2:19 even tells us the devil believes and trembles.

The movie *Left Behind* gives a fictional twist on people entering heaven and on the fate of many who thought they would get to heaven but were left behind with another chance to get it right. The Bible presents truth about judgment day and getting into heaven. Judgment day is final in that no provisions will be made for another chance to get it right. The Bible confirms that "there will be many who tell the Lord on that day about how they prophesied in His name, drove out demons and performed many miracles. But the Lord will say to them, 'I never knew you, depart from me'" (Matthew 7:23). That will be an irreversible and tragic ending for Christians who thought they were heaven-bound.

You see, salvation—being born again—is not found in a religion or in how you look from the outside. It's not about reciting the sinner's prayer or attending church or doing good works or taking part in religious activities. Jesus said, "Most assuredly, unless one is born of water and the Spirit, he cannot enter the

Introduction

kingdom of God" (John 3:3). You know you've been born physically—you're reading this page. But has your spirit been born again "from above"? When you're born again, God gives you a new heart and puts a new spirit within you (Ezekiel 36:26). You are then saved and exhibit a changed life and a personal relationship with God. Relationships matter. This book is about relationship—your relationship with God—which is the most important aspect of your existence.

The bottom line is: In order for you to go to heaven, you must be a "born-again" Christian. Using the Bible as your guide, this book challenges you to search your heart and sift your soul for symptoms of having been born again. Some Scripture verses that will assist you in knowing if you've been born again are John 3:3, 8, 16; Acts 3:19; Romans 10:9; and Ephesians 2:8-9. And 1 John 3 gives the distinguishing characteristics of a born-again Christian. Where do you stand?

Steven J. Cole, pastor of Flagstaff Christian Church, Flagstaff, Arizona, in his lesson on "Facing the Judgment with Confidence," said authentic Christianity has three tests: (1) the moral test of obedience to God's commands; (2) the social test of love for others; (3) the doctrinal test of believing the truth about Jesus Christ. Knowing your born-again status is urgent because it determines your eternal destiny.

The focus of this book is on your "born-again" Christian status and on your personal relationship with God. Is God a distant deity to you? Or is your relationship with God superficial or slight or even stranded? This book shows you how to change that. Have you ever had a personal encounter with God or been close enough to smell the fragrance of God? You can have that experience. See chapter 2. it shows how one Christian did it. Now it's your turn to examine your walk with God. It's time for you to know for sure that you have been born again with heaven as your final destination. Remember: If you want to go to heaven, you must be born again.

Searching for God after Drifting Away is a call to all Christians, an appeal for you to examine your life and your relationship with God. The book exemplifies how I, the author, after living a typical Christian life for years discovered I was not a born-again Christian. Instead I was just going through the motions and following along at the direction of my parents and others. Then, after leaving the nest, I decided to drop most of my church activities and drift out into the world. While out there, I became very thirsty for a real relationship with God and realized that after spending all those years in church I had no personal relationship with God. I knew a lot about Him, but that is not the same as knowing Him personally. I prayed for God to reveal Himself to me. I asked for a personal encounter with Him—to be spiritually born. God answered my prayers and saved me, and a life-changing relationship with God occurred.

Now I realize God's presence in every aspect of my life. *Searching for God after Drifting Away* depicts the highlights of how it happened. "Let the redeemed of the Lord say so, whom he hath redeemed from the hand of the enemy" (Psalm 107:2). This is my testimony of God's love and faithfulness to those who call on Him and to what a difference a day makes with God enthroned on it.

CHAPTER I

Searching For God

"Seek the Lord while He may be found, Call upon Him while He is near " Isaiah 55:6 (NKJV).

The human brain is like a computer with stored information that can be retrieved. The human brain has a memory-storing capacity of about one million gigabytes. (Reber,P April 19, 2010 "Ask the Brain", *Scientific American Mind 21,70 2010*). The writer of *Searching for God* is browsing through her brain's memory bank to retrieve, examine and evaluate the God-memories stored there. Withdrawals from the bank reveal that her God-experiences started even before she was born. This writer's mother, after giving birth to three sons, longed and prayed for a daughter. I am that daughter—the answer to her mother's prayers. I am Odella Glenn, the author of this book.

I was born to godly parents and grew up in a Christian home with a father who upheld and enforced the Joshua standard: "As for me and my house, we will serve the Lord" (Joshua 24:15). My childhood environment included both of my parents and God. It was as if God were the invisible parent who had left instructions for my visible parents to follow. The house rules were to obey God in everything and always do what pleased Him. For the first twenty years of my life I grew up serving and following God. So why did I begin searching and seeking to know God after "following" Him for twenty years? How could I have missed Him? Somehow I did, and the search was on!

I began searching for God, not as an atheist seeking to prove there was no God and not as an agnostic doubting God's existence. I was a longtime believer and church-involved Christian who had realized some pieces to this God-puzzle were missing. But I intended to find the missing parts and complete the puzzle.

When searching and seeking to know God, you go to the Bible first. The Bible contains the very mind of God. There you'll find truth—God's infallible and irrefutable Word. The Bible is the map, the compass to use in the search.

God commands us to seek Him. And the Scriptures give a go-ahead signal to seek God. Seek the Lord and His strength; seek His face continually (1 Chronicles 16:11). "Now set your mind and heart to seek the Lord your God" (1 Chronicles 22:19). Not only does God ask us to seek Him, He checks to see if we are in compliance. "The Lord looks down from heaven on all mankind to see if there are any who seek God" (Psalm 14:2). Isaiah 55:6 admonishes us to "seek the Lord while He may be found; call upon Him while He is near." God asks us to seek Him, and then He rewards and blesses us when we do. Hebrews 11:6 affirms that God rewards them that diligently seek Him. And blessed are they who seek Him with the whole heart (Psalm 119:2). "God is good to the soul who seeks Him" (Lamentations 3:25, NIV). Even "the young lions suffer want and hunger, but those who seek the Lord lack no good thing" (Psalm 34:10).

When we seek God, we're sure to find Him. We have the confidence that if we ask anything according to His will He hears us. And, according to 1 John 5:15, "if we know that He hears us, whatever we ask we know that we have the petitions that we have asked of Him." The biblical character David, a man after God's own heart, is a prime example of one who sought God. His words affirm truth about seeking God. David says, "I sought the Lord, and He answered me and delivered me from all my fears" (Psalm 34:4).

So, filled with the knowledge that it is God's will for me to seek Him and armed with the faith that when I seek God I'll find Him, I press toward that goal. I know I must believe it and not doubt it. "They" said doubt erases faith, and faith without works is dead. I know to pray first about it. "They" said to pray about everything, and in all your ways acknowledge God and He will direct your path (Proverbs 3:5-6).

Remembering and acknowledging who "they" are: "They" are the spiritual significant others in my life: my father, my grandmother and other relatives. "They" are also the pastors, teachers and theologians I encounter in various church settings. "They" formed the roots from which my Christian journey started: watering and nurturing the growing seeds they'd planted. I now stand on that foundation and on God's Word as I seek God's face. The Bible says, "If you seek God, He will be found by you" (2 Chronicles 15:2b). And if you draw near to God, He will draw near to you (James 4:8). In preparing to seek and draw near to God, "Remember then from what heights you have fallen. Repent (change the inner man to meet God's will and do the works you did previously, when first you knew the Lord)" (Revelation 2:5, AMP).

"Come close to God, and He will come close to you" (James 4:8, AMP). (Recognize you are sinners; get your soiled hands clean; realize you have been disloyal, wavering individuals with divided interests; and purify your hearts of your spiritual adultery. I prepare to search for God through confession, prayer and repentance.)

Seeking God Prayer

O Lord, against You, You only, have I sinned and done what is evil in Your sight. Please forgive me for jumping the Christian fence "they" constructed for me and for drifting to, and connecting with, the worldly culture, trying to be both Christian and worldly. The Scriptures warn about such behavior. Matthew 6:24 teaches that no one can serve two masters; for either he will hate one and love the other, or else he will be loyal to one and despise the other. First John 2:15-17 admonishes, "Love not the world, neither the things that are in the world." And James 4:4 asks, "Know ye not that friendship of the world is enmity with God? Whosoever will be a friend of the world is an enemy of God!"

Lord, I've been guilty of operating in both worlds. And now my heart and my flesh cry out to You. My soul thirsts for You. Jesus said in John 7:37, "If anyone thirsts, let him come to me and drink." Further, "if we confess our sins, He is faithful and just to forgive us our sins and to cleanse us from all unrighteousness" (1 John 1:9).

Lord, I set my mind and heart toward seeking Your face. Search my heart, and by Your grace and mercy, forgive all my sins. Create in me a pure heart, and please reveal Yourself to me. I want to have an up-close and personal relationship with You.

Hear my prayer, O Lord. Do not hide Your face from me or turn Your servant away in anger, lest I be like those who go down into the pit.

Thank You, Father God, for answering this prayer. In Jesus' name I pray, amen.

Shortly after my prayer of repentance I heard God say to me in my spirit, "You shall seek Me, and find Me, when you search for Me with all your heart." I recognized those words. That's Jeremiah 29:13. God's Word was alive and speaking to me. I acknowledged. The Bible states that the word of God is living and active, sharper than any two-edged sword (Hebrews 4:12, ESV).

I launched my search for God, and with His help I expected to find Him. And on purpose I wasn't telling a soul. I didn't want my search-for-God decision to be questioned or commented on, nor the progress monitored by anyone. "They" had already said enough. Now I only wanted to know God's perspective on my decision and experience a one-on-one encounter with Him. This search was between God and me—period! I increased my Bible-study time, intensified my prayers, deepened my meditations and praise and worship time, attempting to know God. In further preparation for knowing God, I avoided or eliminated whomever or whatever distracted or was an obstacle to seeing God. I spent much of my time with Christians, in church activities and in church services. I expected to find God in church because the Bible says God is the head of the church and the head of all things in the church (Ephesians 1:22). And any believer is a member of His body (Ephesians 5:30).

My search for God was set in motion as I attended churches—a number of them—trying to find the "right" one. Then I tried other denominational and non-denominational churches—several of them without experiencing God. The churches I attended varied in protocol, temperament and size. I experienced some lengthy, fiery, drum-beating dancing and shouting services. And in contrast some brief low-key, non-emotional services where the piano or organ was the only praise instrument. The congregation sizes varied from meager to mega. I was gaining more knowledge about God as I attended different churches and denominations. But I was no longer just seeking knowledge about God. Knowing about God is not the same as knowing God. I sought to know God—not as a distant deity. I wanted to experience God and have an up-close relationship with Him.

I was becoming weary of attending so many churches, sometimes two in one Sunday. I was all churched out. But God directs us to assemble together to worship Him in spirit and in truth. And God commands: "Don't stop meeting together with other believers, which some people have gotten in the habit of doing. Instead, encourage each other, especially as you know the day of the Lord's coming is getting closer" (Hebrews 10:25). So I decided to focus on attending just one church. Surely I could find God in church. Christ is the head of the church, which is His body (Colossians 1:18, NLT). Anyone who believes is part of the body of Christ. Christ is also head over all things in the church (Ephesians 1:22). And He said, "For where two or three are gathered together in my name, there am I in the midst of them" (Matthew 18:20). So I knew that in due season I would reap a harvest of experiencing God if I didn't give up. I still believed and expected to experience God—in His timing.

CHAPTER II

Hearing God's Voice

"My sheep hear my voice, and I know them, and they follow me" (John 10:27).

One morning, as I was doing my Saturday housecleaning chores, I sensed a lift in my spirit—not that it was down. But for no apparent reason I was having a feeling of exhilaration, a feeling of expectancy. I knew the housecleaning chores couldn't be generating such feelings. Anyway, I continued my chores, but my mind was now focused more on what I was feeling than on what I was doing.

After a few more minutes of cleaning, I became aware of a sweet, rose-like scent invading the atmosphere. "Uh-m, that's the same scent I experienced a few times while I was in meditation," I said. Curious about the unexplained fragrance, I stopped cleaning and moved about the house, inhaling deeply, as I tried to figure out where this scent was coming from. I could not pinpoint the smell, or its source, but I kept moving until suddenly I was stopped in my tracks.

I heard someone's voice. I was at home alone, but I heard a voice. I didn't see anyone, but a voice out of nowhere said, "Be still and know that I am God." I was standing beside the couch and somehow managed to sit down. And I still heard the words reverberating through my head like an echo: "Be still and know that I am God." Whoa! I was on the couch breathless, speechless and motionless for a few moments. When I was able to respond I cried out, "Oh! Yes, God!" I was in awe as I realized that Almighty God Himself, Creator of the universe, had just spoken to me audibly! What a voice! My prayer petition, "Lord, reveal Yourself to me," had just been answered. It was amazing! It was incredible! God is awesome!

I got up from the couch and walked through my house, thanking and praising God for revealing Himself to me. After a few minutes I went to the telephone and made a long-distance call to my father to reconnect with my spiritual roots. As I dialed his number, I thought about my grandmother. She and my dad were the ones who first taught me about God. I grew up hearing them talk about when they heard God's audible voice. God's audible message to my father was: "My goodness and mercy shall follow you for the rest of your days." He received that word on becoming a young father. And now three generations later I heard God's audible voice. Too bad my grandmother wasn't here to hear my story. She passed away some years ago at the age of ninety-six.

My father finally answered the phone, and I told him my story. I cried and talked as if no listener was on the other end. Whenever my father could get a word in he did, and he told me among other things that I could find God's exact words in Psalm 46:10. When I heard that, I said, "Let me call you right back." I got my Bible in several versions to see what God said to me. God's audible words lined up perfectly with His written words in the Bible. I checked for meaning in the Bible concordance and in various commentaries so I could have a clear understanding of God's words and obey them.

In consulting the verse-by-verse Bible commentary, I discovered that "be still" means to cease striving and know He is God. Albert Barnes's *Notes on the Whole Bible* indicate that "be still" means to be relaxed; not putting forth exertion; and being without anxiety about the issue. I also found that "Be still and know that I am God" has similar meaning to Exodus 14:13: "Stand still and see the salvation of God" (Moses' command to the Israelites at the Red Sea).

Regarding the interpretation for "know that I am God," I searched through Bible Commentaries. I found that , "You cannot know this deep and eternal truth unless you are still. If you keep the waters of your spirit in continual stir, you will see nothing in them or only the reflections of your own perturbed self."(Maurice, F.D. "Psalm 46:10" *The Biblical Illustrator.* www.Studylight.org/Commentaries). Another writer explains that some forms of knowledge necessitate stillness. Self-knowledge and God-knowledge can never be had until we have learned to be still. And he adds that knowing God does not come from effort. It comes from reposefulness. (Thomas, R. "Psalm 46:10" *The Biblical Illustrator.* It was interesting to see that God revealed Himself to me at a time when I wasn't even attempting to find Him. I wasn't in church or praying or meditating or even reading the Bible. God came to me without any effort on my part and when I least expected Him. An author/evangelist, once said, "Jesus rarely comes when we expect Him, and always in the most illogical connections. And the only way a worker can keep true to God is by being ready for the Lord's surprise visits." (Chambers,O. "Our Lord's Surprise Visits." *WisdomFrom Oswad Chambers* https://Utmost.org) I was reminded that when Jesus comes back to this earth it will be "in a moment, in the twinkling of an eye" (1 Corinthians 15:52). And no one knows just when, not even the Son (Matthew 24:36).

I think I understand God's message to "be still and know that I am God." Running from church to church and switching from one denomination to the next was not how to find God. And I believe God wanted me to stop it. Sorry, Lord. I wasted a few years doing that, and it was unproductive. Truth has revealed that God is not just "out there" somewhere. God does not live in temples made with hands (Acts 7:48). Every believer is a temple of God in which His Spirit dwells. The Creator and God of the universe have chosen to live in the hearts of believers (1 Corinthians 3:16). Knowing and experiencing God are through the heart—the spirit.

My mind kept flashing back to hearing God's voice and to the sweet fragrance that preceded it. God's voice is unlike any I've ever heard before or since. I'm unable to describe it. But hearing His voice is not like hearing a human voice. I could hear God's words but not just through my ears. His words traveled through my head as an echo. I could also feel God's words like butterflies in my stomach. And I smelled the fragrance of God's presence. Studies reveal that the physical senses have corresponding spiritual senses. I believe that my spiritual senses of touch or feeling, hearing and smelling were used in experiencing God. One minister affirms that physical senses have corresponding spiritual senses.(Baer,Janie."Exercising Your Spiritual Senses", *God's Word Allive,*godswordalive.com). And a Christian's spirit-man has eyes to see in the spiritual realm. Christians also have the spiritual sense of touch and taste and smell and hearing as well. It is through my spiritual senses that I have experienced God. It's a glorious, life-changing experience!

My encounter with God was a great awakening. The encounter transformed my relationship with God from distant to up-close and personal. The encounter gave me a new perspective on all of my human relationships and affairs. And quite often when I become still and close my eyes, sitting or lying down, I see clouds of various sizes, shapes and colors hovering over me. Now I am continuously conscious of God's presence, as He says in Matthew 28:20, "And, lo, I am with you always, even unto the end of the age." With such enlightenment my life could never be the same. Never again would living be business as usual for me.

The stories in the remaining chapters of this book are a few of the innumerable ways in which my relationship with God continues to grow.

CHAPTER III

Halloween Tricks and the Divine Treat

"Therefore I say unto you, whatever things you ask when you pray, believe that you receive them, and you will have them" (Mark 11:24).

It was Halloween night and the youngsters in my family, their friends and some parent-chaperones gathered at my sister-in-law's house for a party. All of the children and some parents were dressed in costumes, including a mask or painted face. The costumes they were wearing represented a variety of characters—from angels, fairies and famous celebrities to ghosts, goblins, witches and the devil. All of the children had a big "trick or treat" bag for collecting treats. Before the house activities started, the plan called for trick-or-treating through the neighborhood. In case you're not familiar, this culture calls for knocking on a door and yelling, "Trick or treat!" Then someone in the house opens the door and drops a treat in your bag. If no treat is given, some trick is done to the house, like graffiti on the walls. But this group was instructed to do safe trick-or-treating as well as "do no harm to anyone's property." Another safety rule was to eat nothing you received until chaperones checked it back at the house. Now that the safety and morality rules had been laid we were good to go.

Everyone—except me—filed out of the house on a trick-or-treat mission through the neighborhood. But I decided to stay in the house and wait for their return. After about an hour of trick-or-treating, they all returned except one child. My husband's nephew was missing. The party suddenly turned into a real scary situation with a missing child. My nephew's mother and the others went searching and retracing their trick-or-treat trail but still didn't find the missing child. A police report was made. And everyone, except me, went out searching. Again I decided to stay home—this time to be still and pray. I was living in fresh wisdom in the aftermath of my encounter with God. And this was a time I should be still, surrender to God and let Him handle things. So I knelt at the sofa and prayed,

"Lord, You know absolutely everything. Nothing escapes You. Lord, give us wisdom in finding my nephew. And protect and keep him safe and send him back to us unharmed. Thank You, Father, for answering this prayer."

I got up from praying and sat quietly on the sofa. After a while of waiting and sitting on the sofa, I sensed movement under the sofa. "Must be the dog under there," I thought. But this was not the case. I could hardly believe what I saw: My nephew crawled out from under the sofa and sat down beside me.

I screamed, frightening him. He asked, "What's wrong?"

"Nothing now," I responded. I took my nephew by the hand, explaining everything to him as we rushed outside to tell the others who were searching for him.

They screamed his name the moment they saw him, and he knew why. He got a chance to tell his side of the story. "I was tired and sleepy and didn't want to go trick-or-treating. So, after the first house stop, I sneaked away, came home and hid under the couch so nobody would see me and went to sleep. That's my Halloween trick."

My nephew had been sound asleep under the couch during the whole ordeal. This Halloween party had some real-life scary moments but ended with joy as we returned to our homes. But the story for me did not end there. It continued.

Now, back at my house, the Lord spoke to my heart and revealed what He wanted me to understand from this lost-nephew crisis. "You thought your nephew was lost, but you were very close to him. He was right under you, but you were not conscious of his nearness. I want you to remember that I am always just that close to you—even closer. I reside inside of you as the Holy Spirit. I AM the very breath you breathe."

I respond, "Thank You, Lord. That's amazing!"

The bottom line to the Halloween party was that my nephew's hiding trick provided an opportunity for me to continue a conscious closeness to God, to getting a prayer answered and to receiving a personal message from God—even at a pagan Halloween party. Or just maybe the Lord Himself orchestrated the Halloween trick so He could provide a divine treat.

CHAPTER IV

The Case of the Lost Keys

"Even the very hairs on your head are all numbered."

(Luke 12:7)

Pushing against the snow that has accumulated at our front door, then shoveling snow to make a path to the driveway and clearing two snow-covered cars are all typical winter morning chores connected with living in Michigan's winter wonderland.

While my husband and son took care of the outside snow details, I was readying breakfast and fixing school and work lunches for each of us. After breakfast, my husband and daughter left for their school and work destinations. A few minutes later, it was my time to drop my son off at his school before I went to work. We gathered our supplies for the day, suited up—including snow boots and gloves—headed toward the front door and discovered the car keys were missing. We searched everywhere for the keys but couldn't find them. This changed our course for the day. My son walked to school, and I called to report that due to an unexpected home situation I would be absent from my school teaching position. After taking care of the absent-from-work details, I continued to search for the keys. I still did not find them. In disgust, I gave up and sat down to regroup.

My mind took me away from the missing-keys scenario, reminding me I was still in my "seeking God's face" season and this might be a perfect time to get still and focus on him. I do believe things don't just happen. They happen because either God caused them or allowed them to happen, and His purpose will be accomplished through them.

As I sat entertaining and meditating on those thoughts, another more forceful thought grabbed me: "Don't just sit there; get up and do something now." Reluctantly I got up and felt prompted to clean up the kitchen, beginning with the breakfast dishes. As soon as I entered the kitchen to clean it, I got a directive from what I perceived to be the Holy Spirit. "Before

The Case of the Lost Keys

you do the dishes, give Trouble some water." (Trouble is the family dog who lives in his house in the backyard.) I wasn't excited about giving Trouble water. I wasn't even the one who took care of him—my son did. And why did they name the dog Trouble anyway? He lived up to his name most of the time, chewing up the wrong stuff and climbing over the fence to get out. He was my trouble this morning. So I put my coat and snow boots back on, got the water and headed for Trouble's house.

As I exited the side door to give Trouble water, I got a thought of caution: "Don't close the storm door completely because one time that door malfunctioned and automatically locked when it was closed."

I felt that the Holy Spirit was leading me and bringing to mind what I should do-step by step. The next directive was "Open the milk chute and place its door between the storm door and the lock to prevent the storm door from closing completely." (My milk chute was located on the outside wall of the house, right next to the side door.) I obeyed that directive because I certainly didn't want to get locked outside. One morning mishap was enough.

I approached Trouble's house with the water, but I didn't have much dog-talk for him. He was surprised and ecstatic about getting attention at this time of the day, though, because normally we would all be gone. I made Trouble's day; he was happy. Now I had to get back inside and make my day work.

To re-enter my house, I removed the milk chute door that prevented the storm door from completely closing. And as I was returning the milk chute door, about to close it, a small voice said, "Look inside the milk chute." I looked in the milk chute and got the shock of my life! There inside the milk chute lay my house/car keys waiting for me to claim them. I grabbed them quickly, looked up toward heaven and shouted, "Thank You, Lord! You've directed me to my lost keys! Nothing is hidden from You! You know all things." I rushed into the house and couldn't stop walking or talking. I kept saying as I walked through the house, "They won't believe this story! Wait till they see these keys! They won't even believe what happened. Nobody will." I could hardly wait to tell this story. I held on to the keys as I went through the house singing, thanking and praising God. Losing the keys and finding them turned out to be the way God revealed Himself to me.

How did the keys get in the milk chute? That was a mystery. This is my theory: My son helped his dad shovel snow and had my keys to clear the snow from and defrost my car. Everything was covered with snow, and my son could have been somewhat overcome and thought that inside the milk chute would be a safe place to keep the keys from getting lost in the snow but then forgot he put them there. My other theory is: Being completely unaware, my son was led by the Holy Spirit to put the keys there in the first place. He was not to remember putting them there or else that would have spoiled the plot. The keys were meant to be lost on purpose, God's purpose. And my son was only used to set up the plan through which God would do the rest by revealing Himself to me. And that is what happened. And to God be the glory!

CHAPTER V

Droopy, Withered Plants on Assignment

"It's not the one who plants or the one who waters...but God, who makes things grow"

(1 Corinthians 3:7, The Message).

In the late fall of the year God revealed Himself to me, a challenging opportunity came my way. The city park initiated a science project: The flowers that had beautified the park all summer were uprooted prior to the first frost and made available to the local school's science rooms for replanting and continued life on the inside. The science teacher at the school where I taught accepted plants and invited other teachers to participate.

Droopy, Withered Plants on Assignment

"Not me," I said. "My plants always die. I can't even grow a potato plant. With my track record I don't want to put the life of these once-beautiful flowers in my hands. Case closed!"

But a few days later I noticed a few unclaimed, abandoned plants still in the box outside the science room. Uh oh! I decided to take some of the flowers without announcing it. I chose the droopiest, half-dead-looking ones because I had a secret plan for these plants. I wrapped the roots in damp newspaper and took them to my home. I refused to hold on to my collection of failed flower-growing experiences. I would look to God, the Creator of all things, who, according to the Bible, has given us dominion over earthly things.

At home alone with the flowers, I reminded myself that I was no longer the same. I'd had a personal encounter with God, and I could do all things through Him. Going to the Bible for assurance, I read, "You have given him dominion over the works of your hands; you have put all things under his feet" (Psalm 8:6). I realized I was the "him" and the "his" in that scripture and the "all things" included these half-dead flowers I was about to plant. And since God specializes in resurrecting what's dead/broken I prayed in my conversational manner, "Lord, I know You are real and powerful; that You can do all things and nothing, absolutely nothing, is impossible with You. Lord, please reveal Yourself through these flowers and cause them to grow. It's in the name of Your Son Jesus, I pray, amen."

I replanted the begonias in three little pots, using the same soil in which other plants had died. I didn't give them plant food or any special treatment. I placed them near a window in my basement washroom. I positioned them so no one who entered the washroom would see them. I didn't want to answer any questions about the flowers, and I didn't want anyone to disturb them. I watered the flowers every week for a while, and then I stopped. For some reason I actually forgot about them. So for a long period the plants received no water. And when I remembered them I rushed to the basement to see how they were doing. As I neared the washroom where the plants were, my heart beat fast and my steps slowed. I cringed as I thought about how I failed to follow through on caring for the plants. I ambled over to where the plants were. I couldn't seem to open my eyes wide enough to see what was before me. Oh! You could have knocked me down with a feather. Those half-dead plants I planted were alive and well, to say the least. They had grown, filled out the pots and bloomed!

"See what the Lord has done!" I shouted.

Droopy, Withered Plants on Assignment

The flowers looked like the painting of a professional artist. God is an artist. His hand has created these beautiful flowers—without pen, paper or paint. The flowers were alive and magnificent! I was motivated to learn more about begonias. While searching for more information about begonias, I discovered there were many varieties. Wax Angel Wing Begonia was the name of the ones growing in my basement.

I had to describe these begonias to explain the meaning of their name. The flower petals were bright orange with a yellow flower in the center. Underneath the petals were thick, shiny green leaves that looked as if they had been waxed. A soft orange-like color surrounded the edge of the green leaves and created a glow that resembled an angel's halo. (Angels have wings and a halo; these flowers had prominent wing-like leaves with a halo effect.) Angel Wing Begonia seemed like the perfect name for them. Their blended colors were iridescent, and their beauty was breath-taking. God had revealed Himself to me again—this time through these beautiful begonias.

CHAPTER VI

Parable of the Lost Gloves

"And we know that all things work together for good to those who love God, to those who are the called according to His purpose" (Romans 8:28).

The Bible dictionary defines parable as a brief narrative story, told with earthly analogies, to illustrate a spiritual truth. In Jesus' public teaching He taught only with parables; but afterward when He was alone with His disciples He explained the meaning to them (Mark 4:34). The New Testament records Jesus' parables about lost sheep, a lost son, a lost coin and many more. I find no parable in the Bible about lost gloves, but this parable is similar to the biblical parables and shows how the Lord teaches a lesson through lost gloves.

Parable of the Lost Gloves

The gloves referenced in this parable were kid leather gloves I received as a Christmas gift, and I wore them every day all winter. You'd get the impression I had only one pair of gloves. One day, while attending a district school meeting, I discovered the gloves were missing. Thinking I dropped them at the meeting, I made a related announcement and checked their lost-and-found station without success. I decided to follow the scripture that says, "Don't worry about anything; instead pray about everything" (Philippians 4:6, NLT). So I prayed about the return of the gloves, ceased fretting about them and left the outcome to God.

This parable could also be titled "The Parable of the Lost Son," because I lost my favorite leather gloves during the time when my son was lost—physically missing. He left home for another one of his overseas missions and had not been heard from in a few months, nor had I been able to contact him. But, as strange as it may seem, as the story unraveled, there was a real connection between the lost gloves and my lost son. Stay tuned.

One morning, toward the end of winter, the office secretary at the school where I taught made an unusual visit to my classroom. "I have something for you," she said, handing me a dirty-looking blob of something on paper towels. Puzzled about what she was trying to give me, I hesitated to accept it. Then she said, "I believe these are the gloves you lost last month."

I took the dirty-looking blob she was holding, examined it and shouted, "Whoa! These are my gloves! Oh, wow!" The gloves were crumpled, wet and muddy, and I barely recognized them. "Where did you find them?" I asked.

"After parking my car this morning," she said, "my attention was drawn to a bundle on the ground. I felt a strong urge to investigate what I saw. I poked it around with a stick and discovered it was a pair of gloves. Then I remembered how upset you had been over losing your gloves and decided they must be the ones you lost."

"Oh, how interesting! I must have dropped the gloves in the parking lot the day I was on my way to that meeting. The gloves have lain on the parking lot all winter and finally became visible as the snow and ice melted, and then you found them and brought them to me. Wow! That's remarkable!"

I hugged and thanked the secretary for getting my gloves back to me. I placed them on the window sill of my classroom so they could get warm and recover from their winter ordeal.

Parable of the Lost Gloves

At the end of the day I smiled as I took my long-lost gloves home with me.

After a couple of days the gloves looked brand-new. They were soft and supple and looked and felt better than they did when I first got them. Originally, the gloves were pale gray. Not anymore. Their color had changed to a deep, rich-looking gray. "Miraculous," I said.

As I finished appraising the gloves, God spoke to me through my spirit. "Don't worry about your son. I'm taking care of him. Just as I kept your gloves during their hard winter and they were returned to you, ultimately better off after their ordeal, the same thing is happening with your son. He will return to you safely and better off than when he left." What a promise!

"Amazing!" I said. And I tearfully responded to God's comforting message with thanksgiving, praise and worship as I anticipated the manifestation of God's promise.

Three months later, as I picked up my mail, I saw a letter from my son. Dropping all the other letters to the floor, I ripped open the envelope with my son's letter and read through it. "Whew!" was my response. I took a deep breath, sat down and read the letter again. The letter contained information about what was going on in my son's life and, most important, the date of his return home. "Thank God," I cried. The letter signaled the manifestation of God's promise was in progress. It signaled that God is faithful and His Word is good. You can trust Him.

A few months later my son returned home. His return home story paralleled the story of the lost gloves. He told about what he experienced while in the foreign country and all the different ways God had kept and protected him. My son's testimony confirmed the message God gave to me. The story revealed that as we put our trust in God, in big and small matters, He is faithful to rescue and deliver us. I believe losing the gloves may have been providential (by or as if ordered by the providence of God), because the lost and recovered gloves were what God used to convey His message to me. One pastor's devotional says, "God is an expert at bringing good out of bad." (Warren, Rick,"AZ Quotes" www.azquotes.com/quote/810572). A n d about the lost-and-found gloves: I no longer wear them every day. They have become my special occasion gloves. I even refer to them as my holy gloves because I received a message/promise from God through them. And when I wear them I feel a special connection to God.

CHAPTER VII

The Bird Connections

"I know all the birds of the hills and all that moves in the field is mine" (Psalm 50:11, ESV).

I have two bird-connection stories I want to share. They follow in the order in which they occurred.

Early one Saturday morning I arrived at San Diego's shopping mall just as it opened. As I got closer to the mall's entrance I noticed a very old lady sitting alone on one of the benches leading up to the mall's entrance. Nobody else was in that area. I thought, "How odd it is for such an old woman to be sitting there alone." While I pondered the old lady's situation, a strange thing suddenly happened to me. I felt something alive land on top of my head and at the same time heard a tweet.

"That's a bird on my head," I said to myself. Feeling no urge to brush it off, I just kept walking toward the mall's entrance door. The bird stayed on my head for a few seconds and then left.

But the tweeting bird came right back and landed on top of my head again. The old lady sitting on the bench shouted, "That bird sure does like you!" And I responded, "I think you're right." After I took a few more steps, the bird tweeted, flew away and did not return. I ran my hand over my head—just checking. Too bad I didn't have a mirror so I could have seen my bird friend. Through it all, I never stopped walking toward the mall's entrance.

I finally entered the mall, but my interest in shopping was completely gone. I stopped at the first snack bar, ordered a juice and sat down so I could think and figure out the significance of this bird encounter.

Now I understood why that old lady was sitting alone on that bench. She was there to validate my bird experience and provide information I could not have had unless someone witnessed it. Obviously, I could not see the bird. I could only hear it tweet and feel its presence on my head. I thought, "This old woman might have been a heaven-sent angel in human disguise. Wow!"

The Bird Connections

In hindsight, I wished I had interacted more with the old lady. I could have asked about the type and color of the bird, which might not have been significant questions. But things didn't just incidentally happen. This experience had meaning, and I had to figure it out.

I associated a spiritual, biblical connection with the bird. The Bible contained numerous references to birds. After the flood Noah released a dove and a raven to determine if the waters had gone down (Genesis 8:7, 8, 11). During a famine when the prophet Elijah was hiding from King Ahab and Queen Jezebel, God used a raven to get food to Elijah (1 Kings 17:4, 6). And after Jesus' baptism "the heavens were opened unto Him, and He saw the Spirit of God descending like a dove and lighting upon Him. And a voice from heaven saying, 'This is my beloved Son, in whom I am well pleased'" (Matthew 3:16-17). I believe my bird experience paralleled that latter biblical example.

I was recently baptized, for the second time, and recommitted myself to God. I believe God orchestrated the tweeting bird that came and perched on my head to show He was pleased about my new spiritual rebirth and recommitment to Him. That was the revelation I got from that bird connection.

My other bird connection occurred a few years later after I moved back to Michigan. It was the Sunday that marked the third-year anniversary of my Bible-teaching ministry at the senior citizen nursing facility.

After ending the ministering session, I gathered my materials and headed to my car on the parking lot. I started up the engine, but I didn't leave. I was overcome with a strange, unsettling feeling of "Don't leave now. Wait a minute." As I was trying to figure out the meaning of that thought, my inner voice spoke. "Roll down your front passenger window." I obeyed the voice and, to my surprise, saw a beautiful bird perching on the rear window staring at me. "Wow! It's a robin," I said. I could hardly believe it. That bird had waited for me at my car, sat quietly while I loaded my supplies and waited patiently for me to recognize it. I was about to miss that bird. I called it a he.

Now here I was face-to-face with him. I made birdie-baby-talk to him. "Hi, little birdie! You waited to see me?" He turned his head from side-to-side as if pondering the question. Then he opened and closed his eyes rapidly, with what I took to be approval. We were actually making eye contact, a bird and I, communicating. This bird acted as if he was my pet, as if we knew each other. After a few moments, I said, "It's been nice talking with you, Birdie-Boy, but it's time for me to go home. You want to go with me?" I began to move the car, backing out of the parking space, and the bird rode with me. Then as I drove forward toward the exit the bird flew away. What a priceless bonus to have waiting for me at the end of this day's ministry!

And what did it mean? I think this bird visitation on my third anniversary of ministry was God's way of showing approval, to encourage and cheer me on to continue ministering and teaching God's Word to seniors who could no longer attend church services.

The birds and I have the same God and Creator and the same Shepherd who sustains us. "All things have been created by Him (God) and for Him" (Colossians 1:16). And they can be used for God's purpose and glory. Birds inspire us to reach for greater heights in life. We are urged to mount up with wings like eagles (Isaiah 40:31). As to my bird experiences, "I applied my heart to what I observed, and learned a lesson from what I saw" (Proverbs 24:32, NIV). Blessed is he who, when he sees the intricacy and beauty of a bird, stands in awe of the One who created it.

CHAPTER VIII

Led by the Holy Spirit

"And your ears shall hear a word behind you, saying, 'This is the way, walk in it'" (Isaiah 30:2, NKJV).

It was Saturday afternoon when I started preparing for a function that night. The first step was to get the dress I planned to wear out of the cleaners. The cleaners closed early for some reason, and I couldn't get my dress. "Um, maybe I'm not supposed to wear that one. I'll just go on over to Northland Mall (a suburb in Southfield, Michigan) and buy myself another dress." So I drove to the mall and saw a parking space. But the Spirit said, "Don't park. Don't go in the mall. Go home."

"What? Who? Me?" I asked. I didn't bother to answer my questions because I knew who was talking, and He was indeed talking to me. I didn't know the reason for these directions. But I obeyed.

I turned around onto Greenfield Road, punched off the radio and quietly headed for home. I drove to the point where I could stay on Greenfield Road or turn onto Eight Mile Road, the quickest route. At this juncture the Spirit spoke again: "Don't take Eight Mile Road. Stay on Greenfield." Again I obeyed.

I drove a few more blocks down Greenfield Road and noticed what looked like a homeless man holding a "Please Help" sign. I was driving in the lane closest to him, and the red light caught me just as I reached his spot. Now here I was face-to-face with this homeless beggar. We recognized each other. He called out my name as he walked over to my car. He was not just some random homeless man. It was Mark (not his real name)! I knew this man. I knew his parents. He grew up living in my neighborhood. As a youngster he spent nights at my house because he and my son were best friends. I had been like his second mother.

I wondered what happened to him and how he got to this level of existence. Shock, embarrassment and empathy were some of the emotions operating here. We talked for a while, sometimes with tears. The red light seemed to be holding for a long time. When the red light finally changed, no other cars were behind me, and we were able to keep talking. I promised to come back in a few minutes with some money after I got change for the only large bill in my purse. Cars were now approaching behind me, and I drove off to get change.

It was obvious the Holy Spirit was leading me to this man for prayer and deliverance.

I saw a gas station in the next block and decided to buy gas there so I would have change and could quickly return to my homeless friend. But the Holy Spirit had another plan. "Don't get gas here. Go to that station near your house where you always go because they pump the gas for you."

Arriving at the gas station to which I'd been directed, I found it very busy and had to wait for service. While waiting for a service attendant, I noticed another car, parked parallel to mine at the opposite gas pump. The occupants, an older man on the passenger side with a young woman in the driver's seat, seemed to be making no attempts to buy gas. They were casually eating as if in a restaurant. I thought it was strange for them to come to a gas station to have lunch.

When they glanced toward me, I looked away in another direction. This happened a few times until I finally initiated a conversation. "You look like you're having a real feast."

Now they perked up and invited me to take some.

"No, thanks," I insisted. I wished I had kept my mouth shut, which is what I usually do when meeting strangers. Then I decided not to wait any longer for service. I would go inside and buy a soda and get change that way. As I stepped out of my car, the couple in the other car lifted up a bag and tray of food and begged me to come see it and insisted they wanted me to take some because they had more than enough. I walked over to their car and saw what they'd been feasting on: fried fish, shrimp and fancy breads. I reluctantly accepted some food. They even had condiments, napkins and a bag for me—carry-out service! While I was accepting the bag lunch, the attendant finally came to my car to pump my gas—perfectly timed for my exit from "these people." I nervously thanked the couple for the bag lunch and returned to my car. With the change and gas issues settled, I could return to my homeless friend.

I drove out of the station, and the Spirit began talking to me again. "The food in that bag is for Mark. It's Mark's dinner." I drove back to Mark's begging location, but he was gone. I circled the block a couple of times then spotted him in another area. I honked my horn, and he saw me. I parked in a restaurant lot across the street and waited while he walked to my car. I asked if he liked fish, and he said, "It's my favorite food." I gave Mark his bag lunch and some money. He stood by my car, and we talked and reminisced over the good old days and exchanged updates on where family members were. He shared about being down on his luck, and I offered uplifting and encouraging words of hope. As we said good-bye, I promised to pray for him and come back to see him soon. In the meantime, I immediately prayed to God for directions on how I could rescue Mark. I made a long-distance call to Mark's brother who said that he was experiencing sleepless nights worrying about Mark's situation. He promised to come and see about him as soon as possible.

    I continued to pray for Mark as I promised—every day. About a month later Mark's brother (we'll call him Dwayne), who lives in another state, drove to Michigan looking for Mark. Dwayne came to my house explaining his concern about his brother's welfare. Dwayne knew exactly how to find me because I was living in the same house in which he would sleep overnight as a young boy. along with my son-friends. I even had the same telephone number that I had when Mark and Dwayne were young boys living nearby. He was aware that Mark had become a homeless street-beggar. Dwayne described how he had recently experienced restless and sleepless nights with an urge to come and take his brother off the streets. I told Dwayne about the Spirit leading me to his brother and how I was praying every day for his deliverance. I told him his coming to rescue his brother from the streets was an answer to my prayers.

Dwayne found Mark at the same location where I discovered him. He picked him up and came by my house, and we sat talking in Dwayne's car in my driveway. Mark didn't feel worthy to come inside and made excuses about why he didn't want to go to his brother's house. The brothers left my house and promised to keep me posted about what happened.

A few days later I received a call telling me all was set. The brothers were prepared to leave Michigan. I bid them farewell as they drove off for Mark's new beginning and a better life in another state.

A few months went by, and the brothers called me. All was well: Mark was healthy and happy again, had a high-paying job, had his own apartment and was back on his feet again. How awesome is our God!

Here are my reflections on the incidents in the homeless man story. God does answer prayer. I am convinced beyond a shadow of a doubt nothing about any part of the story was accidental. I believe the Creator and heavenly Father orchestrated the whole process from start to finish using me, the brother and others to carry out His plans. The Holy Spirit ordered and directed my steps as well as the steps of all others needed in the process. God in control caused all participants to be in the right place at the right time for a specific right reason. And the mission of delivering an ailing beggar from the streets of Detroit to a new beginning of wellness and abundant life in another state was accomplished. This was not the end of my connecting with the former homeless beggar and his brother.

A few years later when my son died, Mark and his brother Dwayne (my son's childhood best friends) drove many hours to Michigan for the memorial. They sat with the family during the service and spoke words of comfort publicly and in private. The brothers also directed a candlelight vigil in our backyard the night of the memorial.

Since that time the situation has reversed. A few years ago I was giving hope and encouraging words to the street beggar. The former homeless man needing to be rescued from the streets recovered, returned home and was now helping to comfort me and my family from the sorrows of grief.

CHAPTER IX

God Communicates through Dreams

"He speaks in dreams, in visions of the night, when deep sleep falls on people as they lie in their beds" (Job 33:15, NLT).

We sleep at night, but the keeper of our souls never slumbers or sleeps. The Bible gives evidence that God continues to instruct and give counsel during sleep. He can and does reveal Himself in dreams. The Old and New Testaments record many accounts of God communicating with and revealing Himself to His people through dreams; of His guiding people in decision-making; showing people how to avoid danger; informing them about coming events. Throughout the Bible, dreams have had a life-changing impact on the lives of God's people and their destinies.

After stealing his brother Esau's birthright and fleeing from his anger, Jacob stopped to rest one night and had a dream. He saw a ladder in the dream extending from earth to heaven with angels descending and ascending the ladder (Genesis 28:12). It was in this dream that God made a promise to Jacob that all the people on earth would be blessed through him and his offspring.

Another important dream of the Old Testament was recorded in 1 Kings 3:5. The Lord appeared to Solomon in the dream and said, "Ask for whatever you want me to give you."

Solomon asked for a discerning heart and an understanding mind—wisdom—so he could justly judge and govern the people. God was pleased with Solomon's request and granted it. And He included long life, riches and honor along with the wisdom. And Solomon became the wisest and richest king who ever lived.

Joseph is one of the Bible's most famous dreamers and the most accurate interpreter of dreams. Joseph's destiny was revealed through his dreams. His dreams affected his relationships with his family and others. As a young lad Joseph was misunderstood and hated, and his life was threatened because of his dreams. As an adult Joseph saved lives because of his dreams and his interpretations of dreams. Pharaoh sought counsel from Joseph about a dream, and a whole generation was saved from starvation (Genesis 41).

In the New Testament God sends an angel to Joseph in a dream convincing him to keep his betrothed wife, Mary, who was pregnant with the baby Jesus (Matthew 1:20; 2:13). And it was in a dream that the three wise men were warned to go home another way to avoid King Herod (Matthew 2:12).

These God-communicating dreams occurring many years ago exemplify how God communicates through dreams. And the Bible says that God never changes. Hebrews 13:8 says He is the same yesterday, today and forever. So I believe and expect God to communicate with me in dreams. The Scriptures support it: "In the last days it shall be, God declares, that I will pour out my Spirit on all flesh, and your sons and your daughters will prophesy, and your young men shall dream dreams (Acts 2:17, ESV). And since God is no respecter of persons—does not show favoritism—I'm becoming more mindful of my nightly dreams and the related Scriptures so I can recognize Him. I stand on God's Word. Scripture affirms that God speaks once, or twice; yet man perceives it not. He speaks in a dream, a vision of the night, when deep sleep falls on men, while they slumber in their beds. Then He opens the ears of men and seals their instruction (Job 33:14-16).

A few dreams I've had testify of God communicating in a dream. In one such dream I could remember only one word of the dream. In the dream I saw a word in print, I heard that word being spoken intermittently throughout the night, and I spoke the word periodically throughout the dream. To whom I was speaking and for what reason I didn't know. That one word was infused within my spirit during the night dream, and upon awakening I just couldn't let it go.

I hurried to the Bible and Bible dictionary and concordance looking for meaning. I found so much but wasn't clear on what to do with it. I needed a "biblical Joseph" to interpret this dream. I went to my spiritual teacher/ counselor and gave her all the details of the dream. She saw the level of my concern about the dream and decided, with my permission, to call her daughter-assistant who lived in another state. The daughter, not wanting to know any details about the dream, wanted to pray by herself and get back with us later. The daughter called her mother the next day to report on the dream I had. The daughter knew the exact same word the Lord gave to me in the dream. We didn't need to tell the daughter anything about the dream. She told us exactly what the dream was about because God revealed it to her also. Now that's awesome, mind-boggling! The Lord revealed to a person in another state what He said to me in my dream. And that one word, by the way, was "strongman"! That was confirmation that, indeed, it was God communicating with me in the dream. And through reading, studying and getting counsel, I knew a lot about the meaning and application of "strongman" in my life.

Aside from the one-word dream, many others have occurred. In one dream I was given a message to deliver to the senior citizen group I minister to. In the dream I was standing before the group declaring what God says about growing old and comforting them with God's Word: "I have upheld you since you were conceived, and carried you since your birth. And even to your old age and grey hairs, I am He who will carry you, sustain you, and rescue you" (Isaiah 46:3-4). I needed no counseling about this dream. I was clear about what to do. I delivered the message to the seniors just as I had done in the dream—powerfully and with conviction.

One night I went to bed in a state of worry, anxiety and disappointment over a particular life situation. When I finally fell asleep, the Lord directed me to Psalm 34:10: "Even strong lions sometimes go hungry, but those who trust in the Lord will lack no good thing."

Upon awakening, I read, confessed and meditated on that scripture. It provided me with the comfort and assurance I needed for starting another day's journey. I have no doubts about it. God communicates with me during sleep. He has often given me a song to sing in my sleep, and I wake up singing or humming the song.

Another dream I had one night centered on a beautifully decorated cake that appeared for me on my dining room table. In the dream I cut a big slice of the cake, placing it on my saucer. After eating one bite of the cake, and in the process of taking another bite, I noticed the cake on the table was beginning to wiggle around as if something alive was on the inside. As I stared at the cake, I was startled when a big rat covered with cake icing emerged through the opening where the slice was taken. "Ugh!" I became nauseous—sick to my stomach—as I realized I had been deceived into eating a piece of rat-infested cake. This beautiful cake concealed a nasty rat hiding inside—nasty but drenched with colorful icing.

"What's the meaning of this dream?" I asked the Lord.

A few days later a real life experience came to me that revealed the meaning of the cake- dream. A salesman came to my door offering to repair my front porch steps and flower brick border that had broken and missing bricks. The salesman gave an excellent price for the repairs and even offered free labor to beautify the front door if I paid for the materials. He promised, "When I finish the work on your house, it will have real curb appeal." This sounded good to me! He displayed a portfolio of beautiful jobs he'd finished, boasted about being a Christian and pointed out that his parents named him after one of the Bible's patriarchs. The repairman's credentials were great, and his price was too good to pass up. So I accepted his offer, paid one half of the costs and set the date for the work to begin.

The starting date came and went without the repairman appearing. When I called him about the no-show, he offered a "family emergency" as the reason for not showing up and set another starting date he failed to keep—another family emergency, he claimed. I was then suspicious of his intentions and began to associate this scenario with the cake-dream. I pressured him either to do the work or better still just refund my down payment. He then showed up, did minimal work on the project and abandoned it. I was unable to contact him—even his phone was disconnected. This "Christian" repairman's promises, camouflaged under beautiful work, were symbolic of the rat hiding inside the beautifully decorated cake. In the dream I was deceived by the beauty of the cake and ate from it. In real life I was deceived by the repairman's beautiful offers and patronized him.

Too bad I didn't make the dream connection before accepting his offers. Too bad I didn't heed the warning in the dream. Too bad, also, that I didn't use my historical method of decision-making: "Let me sleep on it, and I'll get back with you later." By "sleeping on it," sometime during the night or early morning the right answer or solution to a problem would come to me. Either way could have prevented the deception I experienced. My bad! The enemy won that time, but I've been given a valuable lesson on decision-making and plan to become more aware of the significance of bedtime dreams and apply them to my life. It is in the sleep of the night, when the mind and body are still, that God can speak to our hearts (our spirits) and give us His wisdom. Through dreams of the night we can be informed, warned, convicted, consoled, encouraged—and more. I'm convinced it is through our night dreams

God prepares us for our daytime walk. God is in charge of our lives—even in sleep. And dreams are just one of the many ways He communicates with His people.

CHAPTER X

Falls—after Age Fifty

"He ordered His angels to guard you wherever you go. If you stumble they'll catch you"

(Psalm 91:11-12, The Message)

I have experienced a number of falls, as a mature adult, that could have resulted in serious injuries. One such fall occurred one day when I was home alone working at my computer.

The telephone rang. Hoping it was the call I was waiting for, I ran to answer the phone in the next room. But I never got there. Suddenly my legs were snatched from under me like a runner being tackled on a football field. And I landed on the floor flat on my face with my arms and hands penned underneath me.

As I lay there on the floor, analyzing the fall and thinking, "What a strange fall!" My lower body rapidly fell to the floor while my head was held up, supported momentarily, and then softly hit the floor. My eyeglasses were still on my face—undisturbed! That's when I realized the cause of the fall was the computer cord, still wrapped around my ankles.

This was a gravity-defying fall. Was I injured? I did feel pain in my hands, and I was trying to determine where else I might be hurt or if I was able to get up. Then I heard a soft, soothing voice saying, "Get up. You're not hurt."

"Oh, okay," I said and got right up, more puzzled than pained.

I prepared ice packs and went to my lounge chair. As I sat with ice packs on my hands and knees, I realized there was more to the fall than what met the eye. I'm recalling how my head was held up and supported by some force, while the rest of me went crashing to the floor. It was a two-part, slow-motion fall. Impossible? This fall was a case of divine intervention. Who else but God could defy gravity's laws? It's a miracle! I wish the fall could have somehow been videoed so I could actually see how it happened. I know a face with eyeglasses on, bashed to the floor, could have caused serious head and face injuries. But I was protected and spared injury.

What potentially could have been a 911 call was being taken care of with a couple of ice packs.

The next morning I was able to do my usual forty-minute walk without skipping a beat. It's a little miracle. God is good.

I believe the Scriptures contain the explanation for the fall: "The angel of the Lord encamps around those who fear Him, and rescues them" (Psalm 34:7). Scripture also says, "He shall give His angels charge over thee, to keep thee in all thy ways. They shall bear thee up in their hands, lest thou dash thy foot against a stone" (Psalm 91:11-12). In my case, I believe the angels held up my head so it would not crash to the floor. What an awesome Father/God/Protector we have!

The narrative that follows is an account of another fall I experienced one afternoon in my bedroom. A large, executive-type office desk, accompanied by a big chair on roller wheels, sat in one corner of the room adjacent to a door-less (on purpose) closet. The closet housed supplies I used while working at my desk. I enjoyed chair-rolling from point to point in my office.

One afternoon, while seated at my desk, I saw the pamphlet I needed lying on the floor of the door-less closet. I rolled over to the closet and bent over to pick up the pamphlet, and chaos broke loose. Suddenly the chair went berserk. The front rollers raced backward, and the chair catapulted and was momentarily airborne. Then the chair landed on my back and head. I cried out, "Lord, have mercy! Save me!" I had been knocked to my knees in a praying position inside my closet. Was it time to pray or what?

The Bible speaks about going into your closet to pray. (See Matthew 6:6.) But I didn't think this was the way He wanted me to get there. Next time I promised to go voluntarily without coercion. Anyway this became a prayer closet for me. As I cried out to God, I was able to get the chair off me without any human help. I crawled out of the closet without any injury and without any pain. It's amazing how I came out of this fall unharmed in any way. It speaks of the goodness of God. Scripture says, "The righteous cry out, and the Lord hears them; He delivers them from all their troubles" (Psalm 34:17). After giving thanks to God for His grace and mercy, I walked downstairs to testify to my family about how God saved and protected. I called on His name, and He delivered me from a potentially dangerous fall.

In conclusion, God's Word teaches that many who have professed to be Christians here on earth will be disqualified on judgment day from entering heaven. And the Lord says, "These people say they are mine but they do not obey me" (Isaiah 29:13, TLB). "They claim to know God but by their actions they deny him" (Titus 1:16, NIV). "Their worship of me is made up only of rules taught by men" (Isaiah 29:13, NIV).

Sinner's Prayer

Dear God:

I know I'm a sinner, and I ask for Your forgiveness. I want to be saved. Your Word tells us that if you confess with your mouth "Jesus is Lord" and believe in your heart that God raised Him from the dead, you will be saved. I believe Jesus died for my sins and God raised Him from the dead. I open my heart to let Jesus come in and be my personal Lord and Savior. Thank You, Lord, for saving me, amen.

ABOUT THE AUTHOR

Odella Glenn is a retired public school and community educator. She was employed in the Detroit public school system for forty-three years. She served as a classroom teacher and a school reading coordinator and retired as a school administrator. Afterward she became a contracted retired educator and worked in Detroit schools for three years as a teachers' consultant and coach.

Currently, she is a certified biblical counselor who counsels from God's perspective. She is a born-again Christian and a teacher of God's Word. Odella Glenn is a "little ol' lady" with a big heart for God and His kingdom. She is a prayer warrior, a prayer intercessor and a night prayer watchman (divinely called to the fourth watch of the night, 3 a.m.-6 a.m.). She is an active board member of Widows with Wisdom, a support group for widows.

The author's former life passion was teaching school and school administration. She now has a passion for teaching God's Word and for writing and sharing true stories that are kingdom-related. *Wisdom for the Journey,* her first book, and *Searching for God after Drifting Away*, her current book, are examples of how she uses writing as a tool of ministry and a tool to witness for God and to magnify His name.

www.ingramcontent.com/pod-product-compliance
Ingram Content Group UK Ltd.
Pitfield, Milton Keynes, MK11 3LW, UK
UKHW041955230426
12048UKWH00008B/353